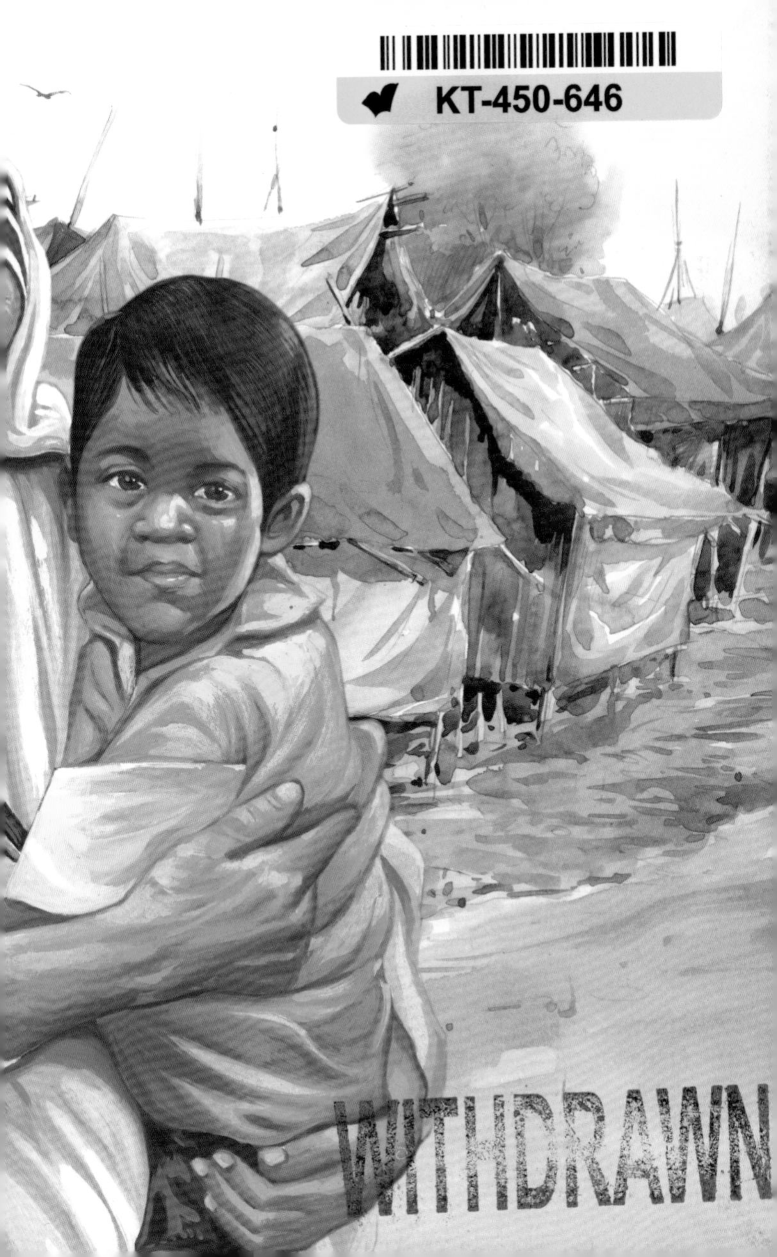

This edition published 2009 by Geddes & Grosset,
David Dale House, New Lanark, ML11 9DJ

Text by Gary Smailes

Artwork by Planman Technologies

Copyright © Geddes & Grosset 2009

ISBN 978-1-84205-668-4

Printed and bound in India

Artwork references courtesy of and copyright © Getty Images,
AP Photo, and Corbis

MODERN HEROES

MOTHER TERESA

A Modern Hero

This is the story of a modern hero called Mother Teresa. Her dedication to spreading God's love and to serving the poor, brought comfort to thousands of people's lives.

Skopje

Mother Teresa's real name was Agnes Gonxha Bojaxhiu. She was born in Skopje, Macedonia in 1910. When she was a girl, she attended regular prayer meetings. Here she learned about India from the letters of a missionary. She discovered that the country was very poor and many of the people had never heard of God. She decided that one day she would go to India to help the poor and to teach them about God.

Missionaries

A missionary is a person who travels to another country in order to preach about their religion — their work is called a mission. Missionaries try to convince people who do not share their particular faith to convert to their religion. In history, some missions have been more concerned with changing people's faiths by intimidation or oppression than by persuasion. Modern missionaries are more likely to try to pass on their faith to others by doing charity work, working to create social justice, improving education and working to help the poor.

In 1928, when Agnes was 18, she found out that the Missionary Sisters of Loreto, an Irish community of nuns, were looking for girls to become nuns in India. She immediately volunteered.

Missionary Sisters of Loreto

The Loreto Sisters is the Irish branch of the Institute of the Blessed Virgin Mary, a religious order for women founded by an English woman, Mary Ward (1585–1645), in 1609. Ward wanted herself and her followers to become "lovers of truth and workers for justice". Mary believed that women should be given the same educational opportunities as men. She also believed that the women in her order should not have to be governed by men. These ideas were shocking for the religious establishment of the time. The Institute of the Blessed Virgin Mary traditionally had three orders, one in Ireland, one in Rome and one in America. Today it has branches all over the world. The Loreto Sisters first sent their nuns to India in 1841.

India

After spending six weeks in Ireland training, Agnes travelled by ship to Bombay in India. She journeyed by train from Bombay to the convent, high in the mountains near Darjeeling. Agnes's training at the convent involved much Bible study, as well as learning to speak Hindi and Bengali. As a novice, Agnes was required to wear a special dress called a habit and to choose a new name that she would be called when she became a nun. This was an important decision and Agnes thought about it carefully. She eventually decided upon the name Teresa, after Saint Thérèse of Lisieux.

Saint Thérèse

Saint Thérèse de Lisieux (1873–1897), born Marie-Françoise-Thérèse Martin, was a Roman Catholic nun who was made into a saint. She is also known as "the Little Flower of Jesus".

Thérèse is best known for her "Little Way". This describes a way of life where small acts of kindness and goodness are more important than carrying out big heroic acts. This was what was important to Thérèse as a way of showing the love of God. She speaks of these good deeds metaphorically as "flowers".

She explained: "Love proves itself by deeds, so how am I to show my love? Great deeds are forbidden me. The only way I can prove my love is by scattering flowers and these flowers are every little sacrifice, every glance and word, and the doing of the least actions for love."

Call Within a Call

In 1931, aged 21, Agnes took her initial vows as a nun. Now called Sister Teresa, she travelled to St Mary's School in Calcutta. Here she was to teach history, geography and Bible studies. She took her final vows in 1937, becoming Mother Teresa. Life in the school was good and she stayed there for 17 years, becoming the principal in 1944.

On September 10, 1946, as Mother Teresa was returning to the convent by train, God spoke to her. The message was clear: God wanted Mother Teresa to help the poor. She returned to Calcutta and immediately began taking food and medicine to the destitute people of the nearby slum of Moti Jheel.

The Slums

Calcutta, or Kolkata as it is now known, can be a wonderfully exciting, cultured and interesting city. It is bustling with people and activity, and it has lots of schools, colleges, theatres, museums, book shops and cafés. But, like many big cities, it is heavily overpopulated and there are not enough places for people to stay. This means slum areas develop. These are areas around the edge of the city that have few facilities and where people make their own houses out of whatever materials they can find. There are about 1.5 million of Kolkata's 13 million population living in slums.

The Archbishop's Three Conditions

Before Mother Teresa could begin her work she needed permission from the Archbishop of Calcutta. She visited him and told him of her plan to live among the poor and serve them. The Archbishop liked the idea, but wanted to know how she would survive with no money. Teresa simply said that God would provide.

The Archbishop agreed to the plan, but he had three conditions:

She would wait one year.

She would get permission from Pope Pius XII.

She would convince ten nuns to join her.

Mother Teresa's First School

In 1948, Teresa replaced her black habit with a simple white sari with blue edging. She lived the simplest of lives, owning nothing and sleeping on the bare floor.

Mother Teresa began her work with a school, but no ordinary school. This was simply a space outside under a tree. Here she taught local children the Bengali alphabet by drawing symbols in the dust.

14

Missionaries of Charity

Classes grew, but the school faced a major problem
– whenever it rained, torrents of mud made teaching
impossible. Teresa prayed to God and the solution soon
appeared in the form of Michael Gomez. He was a rich
Indian Christian, who donated the whole second floor of
his large house to Mother Teresa.

At first, Teresa used just one room, teaching in the day
and sleeping on the floor at night. However, in 1949, a
former pupil asked if she could join her. Mother Teresa was
overjoyed and the pupil became known as Sister Agnes.
Within a few months, nine other nuns had joined her.

In 1950, Teresa discovered that the Pope Pius XII had
agreed to let her continue with her work and she was
allowed to establish her own order, the "Missionaries of
Charity".

Dying in the Street

One day, Mother Teresa found a woman lying in the gutter
in the street. Maggots and rats had eaten away the woman's
feet and the smell that came from her was overpowering.
She was clearly dying. Mother Teresa was overcome with
pity for her. She could see that the woman only had a few
hours to live. Mother Teresa was just a small person, but
she used all her strength to lift the dying woman into her

arms and struggled through the streets of Calcutta to the nearby hospital.

Teresa was very angry, and marched to the City Hall. She informed them that the Missionaries of Charity would help the dying poor, but, in return, City Hall would have to give them a building. That is what happened. Soon after Teresa's visit, the City Hall donated a small building, an abandoned temple in the middle of Calcutta. It became known as the Kalighat, the Home of the Pure Heart (Nirmal Hriday).

Each day, Teresa and her nuns would walk into the slums of Calcutta looking on the streets for the dying. The nuns would place them on stretchers and take them back to the Kalighat. Here they would spend the final days of their lives being comforted and cared for.

Helping a Desperate Man

One day in 1957, there was a knock at Mother Teresa's door. She opened it to find a man suffering from leprosy. She was disgusted. The disease had eaten away the poor man's face, his nose had collapsed and his arms and legs were just bleeding stumps. Even though she was frightened she would catch the disease, Teresa bent down and hugged the desperate man.

Leprosy

Leprosy, also known as Hansen's disease, is an infectious disease affecting the human body's skin and nerves. It has been around for thousands of years. Only very few people are at risk of being affected by it. Even so, people were, and still are, afraid of the disease and of people with it. People suffering from leprosy were at one time sent to leper colonies, though we now know that this is not helpful or necessary. Leprosy causes unsightly skin sores. People with leprosy often lose feeling in their hands and feet because of nerve damage and this can cause them to accidentally damage their bodies. It is not true that leprosy makes bits of your body fall off. People who are at the highest risk of catching leprosy live in areas that have dirty water, dirty bedding, poor hygiene, poor diet and poor general health. These days, there are medicines to treat or even prevent leprosy.

Teresa became determined to help the lepers. She decided to establish a special hospital where the sufferers could be treated in peace. The problem was that she needed money, and a lot of it. Once again, she prayed to God, and this time the answer came in the form of the Indian Prime Minister, Jawaharlal Nehru. He had heard about Teresa's good work. He wanted to show his gratitude and donated 64 acres of land, situated about 200 miles from Calcutta. This was fantastic, but Teresa still needed to build the hospital.

This time it was Pope Paul VI who helped. He had visited India in 1964 and he had been given a large and expensive car. The Pope now donated this car to Teresa. It was immediately sold and amazingly raised $100,000, more than enough money to build her new hospital.

Caring for Abandoned Babies

One day, whilst walking through the streets of Calcutta, Teresa heard the cries of a baby. When she looked, she found a naked newborn, who had been abandoned to die on a rubbish heap. She scooped up the baby and took it home.

Hundreds of newborns were left to die each year in Calcutta and Teresa was determined to help these unwanted babies. She opened an orphanage and placed an advert in the newspaper.

The advert said that anyone could leave their baby at the orphanage, with no questions being asked of them. Soon hundreds of babies were being left. Each one was looked after by Teresa and her nuns. They were saving hundreds of lives.

Mother Teresa's Fame Grows

Her fame began to spread. In 1965, Mother Teresa was well known as far away as Venezuela in South America. The Bishop of Caracas invited Mother Teresa to come to the capital to help the poor. When Teresa arrived, she was saddened by the poverty and immediately set about opening an orphanage. It was here that she also established her first religious house outside of India.

In the following years, Mother Teresa and her nuns would establish houses and hospitals to help the poor in many countries such as Australia, Ethiopia, Yemen and in New York in the USA.

In 1970, Pope Paul VI decided to give her the Pope John XXIII Peace Prize. This brought Teresa further fame. Soon, newspapers and TV channels all over the world wanted to speak to Teresa. She hated giving interviews, but if it raised money for her work then she would do it.

Mother Teresa was now famous all over the world. Thanks to this fame, and large donations, she was able to set up houses and hospitals throughout India. As her work became better known, people gave her a nickname – the "Saint of Calcutta".

More Awards

With the fame came awards. At first, Teresa was reluctant to accept these prizes, but she soon realised that they all came with money. Money that she could use to help the poor. In 1979, Teresa won one of the most famous awards in the world – the Nobel Peace Prize. Along with the award came a cheque for $190,000. She used the money to build a leper hospital.

By Mother Teresa's 70th birthday in 1980, she was one of

Nobel Peace Prize

The Nobel Peace Prize is one of five prizes given to the world by Swedish industrialist Alfred Nobel (1833–1896). It began in 1901, and has been awarded almost every year since. It was Nobel's wish that the Peace Prize should be awarded "to the person who shall have done the most or the best work for fraternity between nations, for the abolition or reduction of standing armies and for the holding and promotion of peace congresses."

the most famous women in the world. Yet she never stopped working to help the poor, always dressed in her white sari with her simple brown sandals.

By 1985, Mother Teresa had opened houses in 50 countries around the world. She was now growing old, but despite her age she never stopped. She continued to work each day cleaning, caring and praying. She survived on only three hours sleep, often writing letters late into the night, only to wake early to take mass at 4.30 am.

Vatican City Soup Kitchen

Teresa had opened many religious houses in many countries, but the one she wanted to open more than any other was in Vatican City. However, to do this she needed Pope John Paul II to agree. Eventually, after much persuasion, the Pope gave in and a new building was constructed within the walls of Vatican City. As soon as it was opened, Mother Teresa converted the house into a soup kitchen. Each night, queues of people would form, all in search of food. Occasionally, even the Pope would visit the house and help them to serve soup.

Heart Attack

On September 5, 1989, Mother Teresa suffered a heart attack while at home in Calcutta. She was rushed to hospital and was very ill. She was in hospital for months and during this time was very close to death. Yet, slowly she regained her strength and eventually was allowed to leave. The doctors told her she must rest – Mother Teresa ignored them. She was now 80 and showed no signs of slowing down. Despite her heart attack, Teresa continued to travel, visiting America, Mexico, China and the Middle East.

Over the next few years Mother Teresa continued her work, but in 1995 she started to become ill again. During this year, she was taken into hospital a number of times. Finally, she was admitted to hospital with serious heart disease and once again she was near to death.

It was decided that she needed an operation or she would die. The problem was that Teresa was old and very frail. The doctors worried she wouldn't be strong enough to stay alive, but they had no choice. They went ahead anyway and Teresa survived.

The Final Day

On September 5, 1997, despite being 87 and in poor health, Mother Teresa was working as usual. In the morning she had mentioned that her stomach was hurting, but she carried on.

She led prayers as usual and attended to the business of the day. However, she quickly tired. As night closed in, she went to bed unusually early. Unable to sleep, she called a nun to her. Mother Teresa was struggling to catch her breath and complained to the nun, saying "I can't breathe." These were Mother Teresa's last words. She died at 9:30 pm.

The Funeral

Teresa's body was placed in a nearby church. For a week, 100,000 people a day filed past the beloved "Saint of Calcutta". Her funeral took place on September 13, 1997

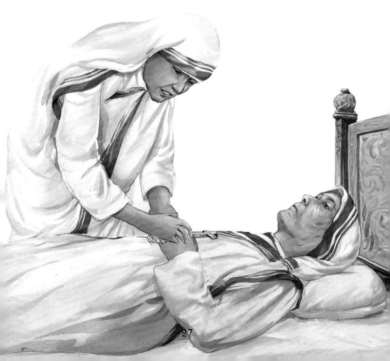

at the Netaji Indoor Stadium. It was held there because the stadium could seat 14,000 people. Teresa's body was driven through Calcutta to the stadium. As the open coffin passed, thousands of people crowded the streets hoping for a final glimpse of their "Saint". Among the crowd inside the stadium, were 1,000 sisters from the Missionaries of Charity, as well as kings, queens and prime ministers from 43 countries. After a four-hour service, the coffin was slowly carried from the stadium. Away from the crowds and cameras, Mother Teresa's body was laid to rest in a private crypt at her home.

A Modern Hero

Mother Teresa is one of the most admired and loved women of the 20th century. She grew from being an ordinary and quiet young girl, to a world-famous icon of peace and love. Agnes Gonxha Bojaxhiu's dream was to serve God. She achieved so much more than this. When Mother Teresa died in 1997, she left behind thousands of houses and hospitals that will go on saving people's lives far into the future. Mother Teresa's passion to spread God's love, and her own hard work and sacrifice, have made the world a better place.